R.E.W.I.R.E.

SIX SIMPLE STEPS TO ACHIEVE YOUR GOALS

YESENIA MIRANDA GIPSON

Copyright 2021 by Yesenia Miranda Gipson

All rights reserved

It is not legal to reproduce, duplicate, or transmit any part of this document in either electronic means or printed format. Recording of this publication is strictly prohibited.

ISBN 978-1-7365888-0-2 (paperback)
ISBN 978-1-7365888-1-9 (ebook)

Published by Yesenia Gipson
P.O. Box 1069
Riverside, CA 92502

For signed copies, bulk orders, or requests for speaking engagements, contact the author at
ygipson@letsallrewire.com
HTTP://LETSALLREWIRE.COM

Editor: Margaret A. Harrell, https://margaretharrell.com
Cover designer: Yesenia Miranda Gipson

To all the wonderful people (so many to name, but you all know who you are) in my life who have loved and supported me, cheered me on and continue to do so. To my mother, Barbara, for always reminding me that I am capable, worthy, and deserving of all my heart's desires. To my sister, Diana, for being my sounding board, my ride or die, my confidante. To Elias, my first child, you taught me how to be a mother and what unconditional love means. The moment I met you, I loved you as if I had birthed you. To my son, Javier, who taught me about a love like no other. You are my inspiration, my reason for everything I do in life, and my constant reminder that I am always being watched and emulated, so I must always stay on my toes. To my husband, Deshon—despite our ups and downs, you have supported me and my crazy for twenty-five years, with love, grace, and loads of patience. Thank you.

Thank you for purchasing my book and investing in yourself

Expect great results as long as you make the commitment to yourself, the process, and put in the work.

For downloadable worksheets, pledge forms, merchandise, and more visit:

HTTP://LETSALLREWIRE.COM

Here's your chance to win 2-VIP tickets to a live event (TBD) with the author, Yesenia Gipson. Get the red-carpet treatment and a Swag Bag full of wonderful gifts and goodies. All you have to do is

Leave a review on Amazon after you have finished reading the book.

Post a picture with your copy of R.E.W.I.R.E. to Instagram & Facebook with hashtag **#letsallrewire**

Tag author on Instagram—@yeseniamg1 and @letsallrewire

CONTENTS

Introduction   ix

The Pledge   1
1. Reflect   7
   NOTES   13
2. Envision   15
   NOTES   19
3. Write It   21
   NOTES   23
4. Include   25
   NOTES   35
5. Review   37
   NOTES   41
6. Execute   43
   NOTES   45
   Epilogue/Conclusion   47

The R.E.W.I.R.E. Pledge   51
Acknowledgments   63
About the Author   65
Thank You   69

INTRODUCTION

> *There's only one way to eat an elephant: a bite at a time.*
>
> — DESMOND TUTU

What does that quote actually mean? It means that when we find ourselves in circumstances that seem daunting, overwhelming, or complex and a solution seems impossible, take that circumstance and break it down into small, manageable tasks and tackle each task one at a time. Doing it this way will lessen the pressure of trying to solve everything at once and provide a peace to focus on the task at hand; thus, ensuring proper thought, planning, and execution of the solution.

Introduction

R.E.W.I.R.E. is a tool that I created to help me cope with the many circumstances I have encountered. Especially during the COVID-19 pandemic, it has allowed me to prioritize and manage my time for productivity. During these past few months, I have been able to learn a new language, grow an herb and vegetable garden, with some flowers thrown in there. I have made some clothes (using ready-made patterns, of course) and jewelry, read a few books, binge-watched some shows, cooked more meals than in my entire forty-nine years combined (exaggerating a bit), hosted my monthly virtual Coffee & Cents event, started writing a novel, and put this process on paper, which I will soon be teaching virtually.

While there are six simple steps in this process, it will require commitment and some careful thought. The process is a combination of things I've learned along the way from some of my greatest mentors. Mentors like Tony Robbins, Les Brown, Mel Robbins, Lisa Nichols, and so many more.

R.E.W.I.R.E is an acronym for the steps in the process, which stands for Reflect, Envision, Write It, Include, Review, and Execute. The steps in the

Introduction

process are really that simple. "Then why aren't more people doing it?" you ask. Well, for one, because I'm just now revealing this process to the public. And two, it takes effort and commitment. People get all scared and jittery when they hear *effort* and *commitment* because it means accountability! And accountability means having to look at yourself in the mirror every day and ask, "Have I put forth enough effort and stayed committed to my promise?" And respect yourself after answering.

Think about it. How many New Years have you made a resolution and stuck with it? How often have you set a goal for yourself you failed to reach? Odds are more than you care to admit. Well, at least for me. And why is that? The answer is, people do not commit to processes that require too much effort and commitment because they do not have a strong motivator. They do not have a strong enough reason to keep them focused and see a plan through. It's like a bull chasing your behind or a carat dangled in front. Which of the two is the greater motivator for you to move (take action)? Some will say that the carat dangled in front is the best motivator because it represents the prize at the end. However, the bull is the best motivator because it represents the end of

Introduction

your life, the end of your dream if you let it catch you. So, find your bull, your motivator, and let's get started!

THE PLEDGE

> *A pledge that has been taken but needs motivation to continue cannot be sustained.*
>
> — Prashant Agarwal

Before I delve into the pledge, have you found your bull?

"What is a bull again?" you ask. In case you skipped over the introduction, which many do when reading books including myself, here it is.

Many have made New Year's resolutions and set goals but failed in achieving them due to not having the right motivator. What will spring you into immediate action in this scenario: a bull chasing your behind or a diamond carat dangling ahead?

Let me paint the picture for you. You and your best pal Aries, a Yorkie-Chihuahua mix, are sitting in a park having a picnic and enjoying a warm sunny day. A rabbit hops across the edge of your picnic blanket with a dollar bill stuck to its back. Short of holding Aries back so he doesn't chase the rabbit, are you going to spring up to chase the dollar bill? Probably not. You may think about it, depending on how low on funds you are. LOL. My bet is that you aren't phased one bit.

Now, let me paint you another picture. Same park, picnic, warm sunny day and Aries. All of a sudden you see a bull charging straight for you and Aries. How fast are you springing up now? I guarantee you won't even think twice to get out of Dodge. And if Aries ain't on board with getting out of Dodge, you will remember him with love. (I hope you know this is a funny. Go ahead and laugh.)

If you chose as your motivator the bull, not the carat (dollar bill on rabbit), you are absolutely right. A bull chasing your behind will definitely spring you into action immediately. When things need to get done, sitting around lollygagging isn't going to help.

R.E.W.I.R.E.

You need that bull to chase you around the block to get your energy flowing. And yes, I said lollygagging.

Let me share my bulls with you. Yes, I have a couple. I have no time to waste or slack off because if I do either, the other will get me. My first bull is my son, Javier. He is my miracle and the greatest testament to God's existence. For over thirteen years, doctors kept telling me that there was nothing physically wrong, I just did not get pregnant. Test after test revealed nothing, yet year after year, no pregnancies. And then, through a series of odd events, I came across USC Fertility. I was thirty-seven years old, and with one final attempt in me, I made my appointment. Soon I had my first try with in-vitro fertilization (IVF) and through the doctors, God delivered my miracle, my Javier. He is THE love of my life, my motor, my air, my heartbeat, my everything! From the moment I knew I was pregnant with him, I reshaped my life to center on him. All I have done and continue to do is because of him and for him. There is nothing he will ever want for that I won't figure out how to get it to him. Don't get it twisted. I'm still very much a Latina mom. He may be spoiled (not a brat), but he gives respect, has values, and earns his keep.

My second bull is self-sufficiency. I never want to depend on any man or company for my finances. I was married, and my ex-tried to break me in our divorce; a common expression of a wounded ego that can no longer control what he believes to be his possession. That's a whole story in itself. I'll save it for one of my next books.

I have also seen how many have given their lives to corporations, only to be laid off and dismissed without a care as to how that decision impacts an entire family's way of life. And that is something I cannot allow myself to be a part of. I will give my time, knowledge, expertise, and energy to myself, my family, and my own company. My successes and my failures will be my own. My legacy will be mine and, on my terms, to create and pass on to my son and future generations.

So, now that I have explained it, I'll tell you again. Find your ***bull*** and let's get started!

Let's discuss The Pledge. This is where you make a commitment to yourself and to your bull! Yes, it is a contract between you and you for you.

You are going to pledge to yourself, and your bull, that you will be ***fully committed*** to this process for the specified duration you deem fitting to achieve your goal. You will pledge that come hell or high water you will not get distracted. Nor will you stray from your plan. You are going to pledge allegiance to yourself, your bull, and this process.

Once you have completed and signed your pledge, you will make four copies and do as follows:

- Copy 1—Tape it on your mirror. This is the mirror that you look into every morning and every night. If you don't have one, find one and designate it as your Morn/Nite Mirror
- Copy 2—Tape it to your laptop (on the outside top) or computer desk (under your keyboard)
- Copy 3—Place it in your wallet or phone case
- Copy 4—Instructions will be given in Chapter 5

Note: Do not complete your pledge until you have finished reading the entire book. It's a very small book, an easy read. It will take less than one hour to read.

The Pledge form is located at the end. I have included several cuttable pledge forms for your convenience.

1
REFLECT

> *Time spent in self-reflection is never wasted —it is an intimate date with yourself.*
>
> — Paul TP Wong

Merriam-Webster defines reflection as *the production of an image by or as if by a mirror*. It also defines it *as a thought, idea, or opinion formed or a remark made as a result of meditation*. And that is exactly what you are going to do in the first step of the R.E.W.I.R.E. process, Reflect.

Reflection is an extremely powerful tool. Reflection is done in silence and solitude. In other words, it's done in meditation with little to no disruptions. This allows you to look deep into yourself (self-reflection) and understand how you "operate." You come to learn where your weaknesses and strengths lie. Reflecting helps with identifying any negative thoughts or limiting beliefs you may have so that you can transform them into positive thoughts and beliefs of abundance.

Reflection allows you to look back and analyze the processes and outcomes of the past. Even decipher the reasons why you decided, chose, or reacted the way you did in certain situations. You are able to see where things could have gone better or worse or where they were just right. It gives you the ability to think critically and calmly. Because when you reflect, it is usually on what *was*, past tense; there is no changing the past now. However, what arises from reflecting are solutions and ideas that are genuine, pure; they come from a place of peace and tranquility. And so you can now apply those solutions and ideas to the future as needed.

Every aspect of your life deserves to be reflected upon. This includes reflecting on relationships with family and friends, health, career, spirituality, personal growth, education, and finance (if I missed any, just add them to your list). List the ones you feel need improvement or need to be taken to the next level and then prioritize them. Prioritizing will reveal what is most important to you. Once you have your prioritized list, begin tackling them one by one. Understand that this is *your* journey; your R.E.W.I.R.E. journey. You ride this journey however you want. But once you make your selection, you must commit to it till the end. Remember that pledge?

Like meditation, reflection requires a few things in order for it to work. The first thing you need is clarity on what you will be reflecting on. For instance, your relationship with your sibling has been strained for a while and your goal is to mend things so that you can rebuild that relationship. You will want to know exactly how you want that relationship to be. Do you want to add boundaries? Are you needing/requiring an apology to move forward?

Next, you will need to find a quiet place where you can be alone without interruptions. Maybe a place that brings you peace and tranquility. The beach is always that place for me. I prefer the beach at sunrise when I need to reflect on something big or difficult. You want to dedicate no less than ten minutes to your reflection. And you want to have pen and paper to jot down anything that comes up for you during this time. There may be feelings, ideas, or maybe nothing at all. But you want to be prepared.

When you have found your peaceful place, begin to reflect. Start from the beginning. If using the sibling example above, start reflecting on how and when did the relationship begin to strain. Think about all that has taken place since and what you contributed to the tension. Be present in every moment you are reflecting on and identify any feelings surfacing, any A-HA moments, any ideas.

Here are some questions to ask yourself throughout this process:

- What initially happened? What could I have done differently? What is the underlying issue? What has been my contribution (negative or positive)?
- When did it first happen? When do I want to start to change things?
- Why did it happen? Why did I react that way? Why did I feel that way? Why do I still feel this way?

- Where do I want this relationship to go? Where is it heading?
- How should I approach it? How will mending the relationship affect me/us?

These are just some questions to get you started. Remember to be present in the moment and to jot anything down that comes up for you or that you feel are important.

NOTES

2

ENVISION

> *What you envision in your mind, how you envision the world around you is of great importance because those things become your focus.*
>
> — Dr. Eric Thomas (ET, the Hip Hop Preacher)

To envision is to imagine your vision, accompanied by the emotions you will have after reaching the desired outcome—and experiencing those emotions as if the outcome had already happened. Let me explain. If my goal is to lose thirty pounds to once again fit into my favorite dress and wear it at my high school's fortieth reunion, I need to envision that.

Here is how the process of Envision works. I'm going to ask myself, "why that dress?" My answer is "because it fit perfectly and flattered my figure. In this dress I felt amazing and confident. Not to mention, all the compliments I received when I wore it." I'm going to close my eyes, envision myself in that dress, and feel all the wonderful and inspiring emotions I felt when I used to wear it.

Again, I'm going to close my eyes as I envision myself walking into my fortieth reunion in that dress, feeling strong and confident. I'm in my best shape, looking and feeling amazing. I exude confidence as I stand tall with my head held high. Are heads turning, jaws dropping? Am I approachable? Are smiles being sent my way? Am I getting the reaction I was looking for? I'm envisioning that reaction. How do I feel as I'm reconnecting with old friends? Am I speaking confidently with them? Am I being receptive and intentional with my connections? Am I enjoying myself and having fun? How positive is this experience? I'm envisioning all the desired outcomes and feelings.

You must envision everything exactly as you want it to be and feel exactly as you want to feel as if it has already happened. When you have committed to the envisioning process, it should feel like you just woke up from the realest dream.

Now that you know how to properly envision, commit to envisioning at least twice a day. Once in the morning and again before bed. Create a habit of it. The more you practice, the more real and attainable it becomes, the harder you'll work towards your goal, and the closer you'll get to achieving it.

NOTES

3
WRITE IT

> *People who very vividly describe or picture their goals are anywhere between 1.2 to 1.4 times more likely to successfully accomplish their goals than people who don't.*
>
> — MARK MURPHY

Let's talk about the science behind writing things down. The science explains there is external storage and there is encoding.

In the external-storage process, the information is stored externally, as in writing on a piece of paper or digitally written on a smart device. This allows the information to be readily and easily accessible. Having your goals written down and strategically posted where they are visible assists in visualizing and envisioning what you wish to accomplish.

The encoding process is where the deeper, more scientific results come in. Encoding is the process where things we perceive are sent to our brain to be analyzed. More specifically, the information we view (perceive) is sent to a part of the brain, called hippocampus, located in the temporal lobe. The complex brain structure's role is to learn, process emotions, and form memory.

Writing things down improves the encoding process, increasing the chance of remembering. Neuropsychologists say that individuals demonstrate better memory when they've generated information themselves, such as from word fragments, as contrasted with just reading the information.[1] This is called the *generation effect*. By writing down your goal, you are stimulating the encoding process that allows you to seal your vision.

---

1. (Murphy, 2018)

NOTES

4

INCLUDE

> *The human heart is so delicate and sensitive that it always needs some tangible encouragement to prevent it from faltering in its labour.*
>
> — MAYA ANGELOU

Now, let's add a third and fourth level, to Write It to *seal the deal*. I'll talk about the fun level first. Let's create a ***vision board*** of your goals. In your vision board, be sure to include encouraging and motivating quotes, pictures of the end result (cf., dream house, dream car, picture of your best physical state, united family, pictures capturing happier times in your life you desire to get back to).

Flood your board with all the positivity and motivation you need to help you envision your goals and invoke the emotions you desire to have after accomplishing them.

You want your vision board to be personal, specific, and pleasing. But it must also scare you a bit. Scare in a good way. It must depict your BIGGEST, WILDEST DREAMS. Think and dream BIG. You want a new home? Great! Go find a castle on a hill along the coast of the Greek Isles or a mansion that you feel is way out of reach for you. Put it on your board. Envision waking up in that house!

You want to write a book? Create a book cover with a title and your name as the author. Add a *New York Times* Bestseller sticker on it, print it, and put it on your board! Is it scary? Heck, yeah it is! But how wonderful will it be to write, publish, and have a *New York Times* bestseller? Envision that dream!

Do not limit yourself! Give yourself permission to dream BIG because we have been trained to dream small and stay small. I am telling you that you are NOT small, YOU ARE A GIANT, and only GREAT BIG THINGS CAN COME FROM YOU! *I CHALLENGE YOU TO DREAM BIG!*

Once you have completed your vision board, place it where it is the first thing you see when you wake up and the last thing you see before you go to sleep. Remember, I told you to commit to the envision process twice daily? Well, here is how you will remember to do it and stay committed. You can't say I never did anything good for you. LOL

All right. Enough fun stuff. Let's get to the next level. In addition to a vision board, you will need to create a plan of action to achieve your goals and execute that plan. A plan of action is simply the yellow brick road to your goals. You lay it out, brick by brick, and then you follow (execute) the road.

While it is really simply put, there are some things your plan of action should have to ensure you are successful. Here are the five key items to create a successful plan of action:

- Order
- Completion Date
- Contingency Plan
- Support System
- Accountability

Order

The first key item of your plan of action is to have an orderly sequence of steps needed to get to the finish line. For instance, your goal is losing thirty pounds. The first question to ask is, "How am I going to accomplish that?" You know you will need to exercise and implement a healthy nutritional plan. Now you can either go to a regular gym with a membership fee, hire a personal trainer, or build a home gym. Here are a few sample questions and answers to help you identify the best way to achieve the goal of losing the thirty pounds:

A. What is your budget (how much money can you afford to spend)? **$100 per month**

B. What can your budget afford you? A home gym, gym membership, personal trainer, online training program, a nutritionist and/or meal plan service? **Gym membership: $50 p/mo., which includes online exercise programs.**

C. What will the nutritional adjustments be? **A healthier high-protein, low-carb**

nutrition plan. Does my budget afford supplements? **Yes. A few supplements ($50 worth per month).**

D. What is your ideal/targeted weight? **165 pounds.** Identify total number of pounds to be lost (30) and define by when you want the weight lost. **I need to lose 30 lbs. to reach goal by December 4, 2021 (this gives me 3 months/13 weeks to lose 30 lbs.).**

E. How much weight can be safely lost per week? **1.5–2.0 lbs. per week is healthy and safe.**

F. Based on above answer, how much time will it take to safely lose a total of 30 lbs.? **It will take me 15 weeks to lose 30 lbs. at 2 pounds per week.** Does it coincide with my completion date? If not, how far or close will you get? **It gets me 98 percent complete. I will be shy 4 pounds.**

G. How much time can you dedicate to working towards your goal daily? **I have one**

hour daily to work out and one hour to prepare meals.

H. Is there a workout/nutrition plan that falls within the amount of time you can dedicate towards your goal? **Yes. I can do HIIT (High Intensity Interval Training) workout class 6 days a week for one hour. I found a free meal plan I can follow to help with my nutrition. My budget doesn't afford a nutritionist or meal-prep service at this time.**

Again, these are sample questions to help you understand the process. However, regardless of the goal, the process is going to be either the same or very similar. For the most part, you will need to know what is the goal, what will you need to achieve it, is there an orderly sequence you need to follow, will you need a budget, and how much time do you have to reach your goal?

Completion Date

The second key is the date you will reach/achieve your goal. In the example, I defined a completion date (December 4, 2021). It is extremely important to set a deadline so that you stay on task. If you don't have a defined completion date, you are subconsciously giving yourself permission to procrastinate and not giving your goal the importance it deserves. Basically, you are saying, "I'll get to it someday," and that is completely UNACCEPTABLE! Put a ring, excuse me, put a date on it. Do not take this key lightly and definitely DO NOT SKIP IT.

Contingency Plan

I'm sure you have heard of Murphy's Law. But in case you have not, Murphy's Law basically states that if anything can ever go wrong, it will. So, whenever you set out to do something or achieve anything, you should always plan for the "what ifs"—preparing a contingency plan to address the issue and get you back on schedule.

Knowing beforehand how you will handle adversity when it arises is crucial to your success. In the aforementioned example, my window of completion is really tight. I do not have time to stop and start over again. I am actually short by two weeks. So I need to stay on track without distractions despite any adversities thrown my way.

What are some adversities one may face in a weight-loss process? Well, lack of motivation, body aches and soreness, being overwhelmed with cravings; or pressure to attend social gatherings, stress (familial or career), etc. One, if not all, of those is certain to arise. So be sure to have ways to overcome those adversities. For instance, knowing your "why" and envisioning every day the outcome will help tremendously. If you have a craving for chocolate, do not deny yourself. Rather, take a small bite of a bar —not the whole bar. Or drink some water to subside the craving. Redirect your energy and focus away from the craving, for example, by cleaning or going for a walk.

Support System

Life can be so much better and easier when you have a support system in place. Rally your family and friends and explain how immensely important achieving this goal is for you. Get them to buy into your vision and support you in different ways. Have someone be your sounding board; another be your walking partner; assign someone else to "hang out" and meal prep with you. Maybe one of them will join in and do the process with you. And those that refuse or are unwilling to support you through this, stay away from them. You have my permission to put them on a time-out for the duration of your process (I got your back). You do not have time for that kind of negative energy in your life ever, but especially while you are doing something good and positive for yourself.

Accountability

How will you hold yourself accountable? If you have someone join you on your journey, you can be each other's accountability partners and life will be that much easier. If no one joins you, make your biggest cheerleader and supporter your accountability holder. That person will make sure you are staying on track and keeping your word to yourself. He or she will see you through it and—when having to be a drill sergeant during those unmotivated and difficult times—will not falter. They won't let you quit on yourself.

NOTES

5

REVIEW

> *Review your goals twice every day in order to be focused on achieving them.*
>
> — LES BROWN

Much like you review your daily calendar to remind yourself and make a mental note of what is to happen throughout the day, you must review your entire process. DO NOT FREAK OUT! It will take you a couple of minutes, and it's not as in-depth or as emotional as when you *Envision*. You are simply doing the following:

- In the morning, before you *Envision*, review

your calendar, your goals, your "WHY," and your plan of action. This will remind you why you are doing what you are doing and how you are doing it. Then you *Envision*.

- In the evening, you are doing the same with the exception of one small addition. You are going to reflect on your action items for the day and how well/not-so-well you did with them. If you did well, celebrate your successes, however small they may seem to you. No one gives us any "participation trophies," so we must give them to ourselves. If you happen to do not-so-well, analyze why not and immediately forgive yourself. We are our harshest critic. Life is tough enough and filled with people trying to put us down, invalidate our efforts, and continuously point out our mistakes. Do not join them. Analyze why things did not go as planned so the mistake is not repeated. And then, forgive yourself because you are worthy of it. Love and be gracious to yourself and understand that to be human is to err. Pick up where you left off, making the minor adjustments, and don't skip a beat. Get back on the horse and ride into the sunset … LOL. You get my drift. Once you have forgiven yourself, you *Envision*.

NOTES

6

EXECUTE

> *A strategy, even a great one, doesn't implement itself.*
>
> — Jeroen De Flander

Time to get to work! Have you ever heard the saying "*Knowledge is power*"? Well, that is not a completely accurate statement. Knowledge alone is just that, knowledge. Graduating from medical school does not make you a doctor. It provides the credentials to work in a hospital under the supervision and tutelage of board-certified doctors. You actually have to complete a residency (beginning with a year of medical internship) to become a doctor. You must put your knowledge to work. So, the complete statement goes:

Knowledge + Plan of Action + Execution = Power

Knowing your goals and mapping out a plan of action to achieve them is half the battle. You have set your goals, you have created a plan of action, and you have made a commitment to yourself. Now you are ready to *EXECUTE*. Now is when you take all the preplanning you did and put it into action. This is the part of the process people are referring to when they say they have been through *the blood, sweat, and tears*. This is the time to *roll up your sleeves and get good and dirty*. As RuPaul says,

"YOU BETTER WORK!"

NOTES

EPILOGUE/CONCLUSION

> *I was never a natural. I got there in the end because I did believe that if you work hard enough, then you can achieve a lot.*
>
> — Victoria Beckham

Now that I've covered my six simple steps to achieve your goals, it's time to put what you have learned into practice. There are still two last things I must tell you that are very important in this R.E.W.I.R.E. process. The first one is *self-forgiveness.*

As I mentioned before, we tend to be our most ruthless critics. We allow the voices in our heads to tell us how unworthy we are—that we are not enough. And when we quit, we allow those defeatist voices to be affirmed. I am here to tell you they are dead wrong! You are more than enough! You are more than capable. You are amazing. And you are human. Being human gives you the right to get it wrong sometimes. It gives you the right to pause in your steps. Being human makes it OK to feel overwhelmed. And it also gives you the strength and right to get up, shake it off, and get right back at task when you are good and ready.

If you should falter, miss a day or two, take a long break, change course, etc., you have my most expressed and nonjudgmental permission to forgive yourself. Be kind to your soul and your mind. And then start the R.E.W.I.R.E. process over again. It is OK. This is not a race. It is not a competition. This is your journey, and you walk it however you see fit. R.E.W.I.R.E. is a tool to help make your life easier.

It is a simple acronym to remember. Think of it as rewiring your brain to simplify accomplishing a goal. *R.E.W.I.R.E.*

> **R**-eflect
> **E**-nvision
> **W**-rite It
> **I**-nclude
> **R**-eview
> **E**-xecute

You first *Reflect* on the goal(s) you wish to achieve. If there is more than one goal, place them in order of importance. Once you have selected the goal(s) to focus on, take the time to

Envision your goal(s) as if you have already achieved it(them). Be sure to *Envision* a few times a day, no less than twice.

Write it(them) down. Your brain needs the mental vision and the written part to seal it. It is the stamp on the brain. Create a vision board and include pictures, positive quotes—anything that motivates you to put the work in and stay on track. Twice a day, *Review* your goals and your "why"; in the morning before you *envision* and at night before you go to bed. And finally, *Execute* your plan of action. Get to work. Put your *bull* where you can see it so when you feel like slacking off, you **DON'T!**

The second thing is DO NOT FORGET TO CELEBRATE YOUR ACCOMPLISHMENT! No matter how big or small, celebrate like its nobody's business. Reward yourself with something fun, nice, or even expensive if you choose. As long as it is something you know is going to make you happy because you DESERVE IT!

The R.E.W.I.R.E. Pledge

I, *Your Name*, pledge allegiance to myself and to *Your Bull*, that from *Start Date* through *Completion Date*, I will put forth 100 percent effort and be completely honest with myself and *Accountability Partner*. I will uphold and stay true to my values and BS (*Belief System*). I will remain open-minded to the possibility of readjusting my BS if it is of a negative nature, invalidating my efforts, attacking my self-esteem and limiting my ability to move forward in the direction I desire to go to achieve my goal. And if I should become distracted or stray away from my plan of action, I will *FORGIVE* myself and *RECOMMIT* to myself and the **R.E.W.I.R.E.** process.

Your Signature

Accountability Partner Signature

The R.E.W.I.R.E. Pledge

I, _____, pledge allegiance to myself and to _____ that from _____ through _____, I will put forth 100 percent effort and be completely honest with myself and_____. I will uphold and stay true to my values and BS (*Belief System*). I will remain open-minded to the possibility of readjusting my BS if it is of a negative nature, invalidating my efforts, attacking my self-esteem and limiting my ability to move forward in the direction I desire to go to achieve my goal. And if I should become distracted or stray away from my plan of action, I will *FORGIVE* myself and *RECOMMIT* to myself and the R.E.W.I.R.E. process.

_____

(*Your Signature*)

_____

(*Accountability Partner Signature*)

The R.E.W.I.R.E. Pledge

I, _____, pledge allegiance to myself and to _____ that from _____ through _____, I will put forth 100 percent effort and be completely honest with myself and_____. I will uphold and stay true to my values and BS (*Belief System*). I will remain open-minded to the possibility of readjusting my BS if it is of a negative nature, invalidating my efforts, attacking my self-esteem and limiting my ability to move forward in the direction I desire to go to achieve my goal. And if I should become distracted or stray away from my plan of action, I will *FORGIVE* myself and *RECOMMIT* to myself and the R.E.W.I.R.E. process.

_____

(*Your Signature*)

_____

(*Accountability Partner Signature*)

The R.E.W.I.R.E. Pledge

I, _____, pledge allegiance to myself and to _____ that from _____ through _____, I will put forth 100 percent effort and be completely honest with myself and_____. I will uphold and stay true to my values and BS (*Belief System*). I will remain open-minded to the possibility of readjusting my BS if it is of a negative nature, invalidating my efforts, attacking my self-esteem and limiting my ability to move forward in the direction I desire to go to achieve my goal. And if I should become distracted or stray away from my plan of action, I will *FORGIVE* myself and *RECOMMIT* to myself and the R.E.W.I.R.E. process.

_____
(*Your Signature*)

_____
(*Accountability Partner Signature*)

The R.E.W.I.R.E. Pledge

I, _____, pledge allegiance to myself and to _____ that from _____ through _____, I will put forth 100 percent effort and be completely honest with myself and_____. I will uphold and stay true to my values and BS (*Belief System*). I will remain open-minded to the possibility of readjusting my BS if it is of a negative nature, invalidating my efforts, attacking my self-esteem and limiting my ability to move forward in the direction I desire to go to achieve my goal. And if I should become distracted or stray away from my plan of action, I will *FORGIVE* myself and *RECOMMIT* to myself and the R.E.W.I.R.E. process.

_____

(*Your Signature*)

_____

(*Accountability Partner Signature*)

The R.E.W.I.R.E. Pledge

I, _____, pledge allegiance to myself and to _____ that from _____ through _____, I will put forth 100 percent effort and be completely honest with myself and_____. I will uphold and stay true to my values and BS (*Belief System*). I will remain open-minded to the possibility of readjusting my BS if it is of a negative nature, invalidating my efforts, attacking my self-esteem and limiting my ability to move forward in the direction I desire to go to achieve my goal. And if I should become distracted or stray away from my plan of action, I will *FORGIVE* myself and *RECOMMIT* to myself and the R.E.W.I.R.E. process.

_____

(*Your Signature*)

_____

(*Accountability Partner Signature*)

ACKNOWLEDGMENTS

So many thanks to the most amazing Tias, Tios (*Inez, Yolanda, Altagracia, Nellie, Janet, Rosalina, Victor Jose, Ruben, Buluco, Felix, Daisy, Digna*), and elders (Tio Niño, Tio Didi, Tio Lapaz, Wela Brijida) a girl could have ever asked for. You each have taught me so much and helped shape the woman I am today. Thanks as well to the BEST Primo-Hermanos in the world—Thaina, Maria, Rafael Jr., Francisco Javier, Nector, Geova, Ramses, Gustavo, Alexis, Odalys, Julio, Joaquin, Natalie, Yoli, Thaina Marie, Vanessa, Carlos, 'Los, Lenny, Rosemary, Dinorah, Johnny, and Kathy. I love you beyond words and am so thankful you guys made my childhood amazing and filled it with wonderful memories and experiences. Thanks also to my goddaughter (Yesenia Inez), nieces, and nephews for making me the happiest auntie in the world because you are all the most smart, amazing, loving, and funny human beings on the planet. And love and appreciation, finally, to my "framily"—Sonnia, Cynthia, Michelle, Maria, Laura, Evelyn, Yoya, and Nana. I am so grateful for your love, support, and sisterhood. You are the family I have chosen to share my life's journey with. The universe could not have selected a more perfect group of individuals to have placed in my life.

ABOUT THE AUTHOR

> *The key to achieving anything and everything in life is to go full speed ahead only slowing down enough to avoid and avert the obstacles one will face. Así que muévete, que voy sin brakes.*
>
> — Yesenia Miranda Gipson

A native New Yorker from the Washington Heights neighborhood of NYC, Yesenia was born to immigrant parents from the Dominican Republic. Raised by her mother and "the village" (her family and really close family friends), she learned at a very young age the value of family and hard work. She also learned about abandonment, heartache, poverty, and the significance of money at the age of ten, when her parents separated.

Being married now for twenty-five years, she and her husband have faced their share of challenges, together and apart, throughout their union. From foreclosure—going broke—to infertility and divorce. Fast forward to a son and remarriage, they are stronger, more focused, running several businesses and maintaining the family unit.

Her lifelong dream of being a published author came true in 2016, when she collaborated with the incomparable and amazing Jack Canfield, along with other business owners, on *The Road to Success* Vol. 2. This collaboration earned an award for its National Best-Seller status.

As a financial advisor and business owner, with her thirty-plus years of experience, Yesenia is able to relate to, speak on, and educate families and our youth about a major topic not taught in schools, or at home oftentimes—finance. She is an in-demand keynote and motivational speaker, most recently at the Black Woman Confidential Conference, where she educated women from all over the world about her Four Pillars to Financial Wholeness.

The idea of R.E.W.I.R.E. came about during the early stage of quarantine 2020. When the world shut down, Yesenia was determined to not allow this time to be wasted or let boredom set in. There was only so much cleaning, cooking, and watching TV one could do. And rather than take up gaming like her husband and son, she turned to occupations she enjoyed but had neglected for a very long time, like sewing. Her machine had so much dust that she was amazed it still worked wonderfully.

She started hosting a monthly virtual webinar about finance, Coffee and Cents. During one of the webinars, speaking on how to teach kids about money and give them tips on saving, the idea of putting what she had been doing to stay busy on paper came to her. And the rest, as they say, is history.

THANK YOU

Now that you have completed R.E.W.I.R.E., please share your experience, your wins, big or small. Be sure to also share any lessons learned and the achievements you've reached.

You may share them privately at
ygipson@letsallrewire.com

or you may share publicly at:
@letsallrewire
For Instagram, Facebook, and Twitter

www.ingramcontent.com/pod-product-compliance
Lightning Source LLC
Chambersburg PA
CBHW070655050426
42451CB00008B/356